First Facts®

Expert Pet Care

KU-311-594

CARING

for

Cats

by Tammy Gagne

raintree

a Capstone company — publishers for children

Raintree is an imprint of Capstone Global Library Limited, a company incorporated in
England and Wales having its registered office at 264 Banbury Road, Oxford, OX2 7DY –
Registered company number: 6695582

www.raintree.co.uk
myorders@raintree.co.uk

Edited by Marissa Kirkman
Designed by Sarah Bennett
Original illustrations © Capstone Global Library Limited 2019
Picture research by Tracy Cummins
Production by Laura Manthe
Originated by Capstone Global Library Ltd
Printed and bound in India

ISBN 978 1 4747 6087 4
22 21 20 19 18
10 9 8 7 6 5 4 3 2 1

British Library Cataloguing in Publication Data
A full catalogue record for this book is available from the British Library.

Acknowledgements
We would like to thank the following for permission to reproduce photographs: Capstone
Studio: Karon Dubke, 5, 9; iStockphoto: fridayphoto, 17, kali9, 15; Shutterstock: 5 second
Studio, 7, absolutimages, 6, AlinaMD, Back Cover, 24, Axel Bueckert, 21 Bottom Right,
DenisNata, 19, ekmelica, Design Element, Eric Isselee, 21 Top, everydoghasastory, 21 Middle,
Jorge Casais, 16, Kasefoto, 4, liudmila selyaninova, 11, Oksana Kuzmina, 3, Peter Wollinga,
23, rawcapPhoto, 20, tatianaput, 13, TatyanaPanova, 21 Bottom Left, Utekhina Anna, Cover,
Vasek Rak, 8, Vicki Vale, 18, Zoran Photographer, 12.

Every effort has been made to contact copyright holders of material reproduced in this book.
Any omissions will be rectified in subsequent printings if notice is given to the publisher.

Contents

Your new pet cat

Cats are popular pets. Playing with these furry animals can be great fun.

Many cats and kittens are in **shelters**, in need of a good home. You must learn how to care for a cat before taking one home. Owning a pet is a big **responsibility**. Your family will need to choose a cat that is right for your home.

FACT

There are different types of cats. Some cats have short hair and others have long hair.

shelter place that takes care of, and rehomes, lost or stray animals

4 **responsibility** duty or job

Things you will need

You will need a set of bowls for food and water for your cat. If you have an indoor cat it will also need at least one litter tray and some litter.

Toys and scratching posts will be fun for your cat and may stop it from clawing at your belongings.

Some cats **shed** all year round, so it's a good idea to get a brush for your cat. Try to brush your cat regularly.

shed lose hair or fur
vet doctor trained to look after animals

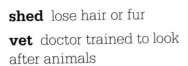

Bringing your cat home

Keep your pet in one room for the first day or so. This can make it feel more relaxed. You can then let it explore your home.

Many cats get on well with other animals. But owners must always be careful. Some cats have a strong hunting drive. They may try to eat smaller pets such as hamsters or birds.

Some adult cats can sleep for up to 16 hours a day!

What does a cat eat?

Your pet needs food made especially for cats. This food contains **vitamins** that keep cats healthy.

You can feed your cat wet or dry food, or both. Fresh drinking water is as important as food. Cats who eat wet food do not need to drink as much water.

Ask your vet if you are unsure about the best type of food for your cat.

Wet cat food can **spoil** if it is left out too long. Make sure you remove any old food and clean your cat's food bowl regularly.

vitamin nutrient that helps keep people and animals healthy

spoil become rotten or unfit for eating

Keeping clean

Cats are very clean animals. They do not need baths unless they roll in something dirty or smelly. Cats clean themselves with their tongues. This can cause **furballs** in the cat's stomach.

If you have an indoor cat, its litter tray should be scooped every day. You'll need to change the litter at least once a week. Most cats will not use a dirty litter tray.

furball ball of fur that collects in a cat's stomach; furballs are made of fur swallowed by a cat as it grooms itself

Regular brushing can help prevent furballs.

Visiting the vet

All cats need a yearly check-up with a vet. You should also take your cat to the vet if it is sick or injured.

Spaying and **neutering** stop cats having kittens. These operations can be done once your cat is four months old.

Your cat will need to be **vaccinated** to protect it from disease. If your cat goes outside it should also be given treatments to protect it from **parasites** such as fleas.

spay operate on a female animal so it is unable to produce young

neuter operate on a male animal so it is unable to produce young

vaccinate inject with medicine to prevent disease

parasite animal that lives on another animal and is often harmful

Life with a cat

Exercise helps to keep your cat healthy. Cats are hunters so they will usually enjoy playing with you and chasing toys. If your cat goes outside, it may sometimes bring home **prey** that it has caught.

Cats can be very affectionate pets. Some cats will snuggle their owners or sleep on them. If your cat does not enjoy being held, avoid picking it up too often.

prey animal hunted by another animal; cats often hunt birds and mice

Your cat through the years

Cats go through different stages of life. Kittens have lots of energy. They need plenty of playtime each day. Adult cats are usually calmer. But they can still be playful.

Cats can have a long **life span** when well cared for. Most cats live for about 15 years. Some have even made it to 20 years.

life span number of years a certain type of plant or animal usually lives

Cat body language

How a cat behaves tells people a lot about what it is feeling. Cats miaow when they want to eat or play. Purring often means a cat is happy. Hissing is a sign the animal is scared or angry. If a cat's ears are flattened on its head it is usually unhappy and wants to be left alone.

Types of cats

Manx

Devon Rex

Some of the most playful cats are:

- Devon Rexes
- Manx cats.

Some of the cleverest cats include:

- Abyssinians
- Siamese
- Turkish Vans.

Abyssinian

Siamese

Glossary

furball ball of fur that collects in a cat's stomach; furballs are made of fur swallowed by a cat as it grooms itself

life span number of years a certain type of plant or animal usually lives

neuter operate on a male animal so it is unable to produce young

parasite animal that lives on another animal and is often harmful

prey animal that is hunted by another animal; cats often hunt birds and mice

responsibility duty or job

shed lose hair or fur

shelter place that takes care of, and rehomes, lost or stray animals

spay operate on a female animal so it is unable to produce young

spoil become rotten or unfit for eating

vaccinate inject with medicine to prevent disease

vet doctor trained to take care of animals

vitamin nutrient that helps keep people and animals healthy

Find out more

Books

Caring for Cats and Kittens (Battersea Dogs and Cats Home: Pet Care Guides), Ben Hubbard (Franklin Watts, 2015)

Kitty's Guide to Caring for Your Cat (Pets' Guides), Anita Ganeri (Raintree, 2014)

Looking after Cats and Kittens (Pet Guides), Katherine Starke (Usborne, 2013)

The Truth About Cats: What Cats Do When You're Not Looking (Pets Undercover!), Mary Colson (Raintree, 2018)

Websites

Find out more about pet care at:
www.dkfindout.com/uk/animals-and-nature/pet-care

Learn more about all sorts of animals and how to take care of them at:
young.rspca.org.uk/kids/animals

Comprehension questions

1. What things will you need to buy in order to care for your cat?

2. Why is it important to watch your cat when smaller animals are nearby?

3. What does it mean when your cat purrs?

Index